KU-424-887

Buddhist
faith and practice

Worship in a Buddhist temple.

Schools Library and Information Services

S00000672531

Bria  agloff

The Buddhist faith

One must believe in certain things with mind, heart and soul; and then live by them in the course of everyday life. Faith is always personal and individual. Each person follows the faith they choose. Here are some main parts of the Buddhist faith.

Buddhist beliefs

▶ All people go through an endless cycle where they are born, die and are reborn again. This is called reincarnation.

▶ All life involves suffering and unhappiness.

▶ Greed is the cause of most of our suffering and unhappiness. In order to stop suffering, we must stop being greedy for too much, and learn to care for everything around us. Once we have done this, we can achieve enlightenment (Nirvana) – a state of being where we no longer suffer.

▶ The way that we achieve enlightenment is by following the Middle Way (also called the Noble Eightfold Path).

This includes: right belief, right aims, right speech, right actions, right occupation, right endeavour, right mindfulness and right meditation.

▶ Love and compassion towards all creatures that live is the greatest good.

▶ The Buddha was the founder of Buddhism. He was a person who found enlightenment and taught others how they could find it.

The ultimate goal of Buddhism is to be free from the cycle of birth and rebirth and to reach Nirvana. We can reach Nirvana by living according to the Buddha's teachings, by meditating, by trying to understand ourselves better, and by doing good works. In this way, we can learn to stop being greedy and learn to love others and the world around us. This brings us closer to achieving Nirvana.

Find out more

Look at the companion Curriculum Visions book, 'Buddhist temple'.

DUDLEY PUBLIC LIBRARIES

L 48006

672531 | BCH

J 294.3

Contents

As you go through the book, look for words in **BOLD CAPITALS**. These words are defined in the glossary.

 Understanding others

Remember that other people's beliefs are important to them. You must always be considerate and understanding when studying about faith.

Lighting incense sticks.

What it means to be a Buddhist

Buddhism is a way of looking at the world to find out the true nature of life. It could be summed up as 'learning to do good; ceasing to do evil; purifying the heart'. It all began with a person called the Buddha...

Where did we come from, why is the world so beautiful, why do people do terrible things, what happens to us after we die, why do we get sick and why don't our wishes always come true?

These are the sorts of questions many people ask themselves. They are not easy questions to answer. For many people the answer lies in a belief in God, the Creator of all things.

The founder of **BUDDHISM**, a man named **SIDDHARTHA GAUTAMA**, or the **BUDDHA**, believed that we cannot answer many of the basic questions about life by looking outside ourselves, and that instead we should look for answers inside ourselves.

Who is a Buddhist?

Buddhists are people who follow the teachings of the Buddha. They try to follow a path (Buddhism) that will help them understand the true nature of life and free them from suffering and unhappiness. This freedom from suffering is called **ENLIGHTENMENT**.

What the Buddha taught

The Buddha taught that all life involves suffering and unhappiness. He taught that existence is a never ending cycle of birth, death and rebirth (called **REINCARNATION**), but that we can break this cycle and become free from suffering and unhappiness forever. The way to break this cycle is to follow the teachings of the Buddha and to look inside yourself to find what is most important.

▼ This woman is making an **OFFERING** of incense to the Buddha.

▶ Statues of the Buddha are very common in Buddhism. The Buddha is not a god, and Buddhists do not worship the Buddha or his statues. Instead, the statues help people to remember the Buddha's teachings.

Buddhism began in India, but today most of the world's 350 million Buddhists live in South East Asia, although an increasing number are found in all other parts of the world as well.

Because Buddhism is a very personal religion, religious traditions and customs can vary greatly from place to place. For example, Buddhists in Thailand have different traditions and customs from those of Tibet and from those in Japan. But there are common threads to them all: a belief in the teachings of the Buddha, caring for the world around us, and tolerance of differences from one person to another.

The most important beliefs can be found in the Buddha's teachings on the **FOUR NOBLE TRUTHS** and the **NOBLE EIGHTFOLD PATH**.

The word 'Buddha' is a title and not a name. It comes from the SANSKRIT word *budh*, meaning 'to awaken'. Once Siddhartha Gautama, the founder of Buddhism, took this name it meant that he was fully awakened from the sleep of ignorance in which most people spend their lives.

Weblink: www.CurriculumVisions.com

The Four Noble Truths

The Buddha thought long and hard about how the universe works and our place in it.

From this he came to the conclusion that there were Four Noble Truths (shown opposite). Understanding these is the first step for Buddhists in learning how to cope with problems in life.

The Noble Eightfold Path

In the very first SERMON the Buddha gave, he used an example of life being like a wheel as his way of making his message clear. We are like a point on the outside of the wheel, going around and around forever.

This Wheel of Law is also called the DHAMMA WHEEL. There are eight spokes on the wheel, representing the Noble Eightfold Path. At the centre is the only fixed point in the universe, NIRVANA. Reaching Nirvana means that we can stop spinning on the wheel and enjoy happiness forever.

The eight spokes on the wheel represent the eight parts of the Noble Eightfold Path. Just as every spoke is needed for the wheel to keep turning, we need to follow each step of the path (see diagram on page 7).

The Buddha taught that in order to follow the Eightfold Path, we must find the balance between luxury and hardship. For example, we should not wear clothes that are too luxurious

or stuff ourselves with rich food, but we should also not wear rags or starve ourselves. This balance is called the MIDDLE WAY and is what Buddhists strive for in everyday life.

The Four Noble Truths

Suffering is common to all
Everyone experiences suffering and unhappiness in their lives.

We are the cause of much of our suffering and unhappiness
Much of our sufferings are of our own making. Things like greed, ignorance and desire for too many possessions, create bad KARMA and cause us to suffer.

It is possible to end suffering
We can stop much of our suffering and unhappiness by not being greedy and by becoming less ignorant. The goal of every Buddhist is to end suffering and to reach Nirvana. Nirvana is not a place, it is a state of being where there is no suffering or unhappiness. Reaching the state of Nirvana is also called 'achieving enlightenment'.

Everyone can be enlightened
The fourth Noble Truth tells us that, with the help of the Buddha's teachings, it is possible for everyone to reach Nirvana, or achieve enlightenment. The way to do this is to follow the Noble Eightfold Path.

The Noble Eightfold Path

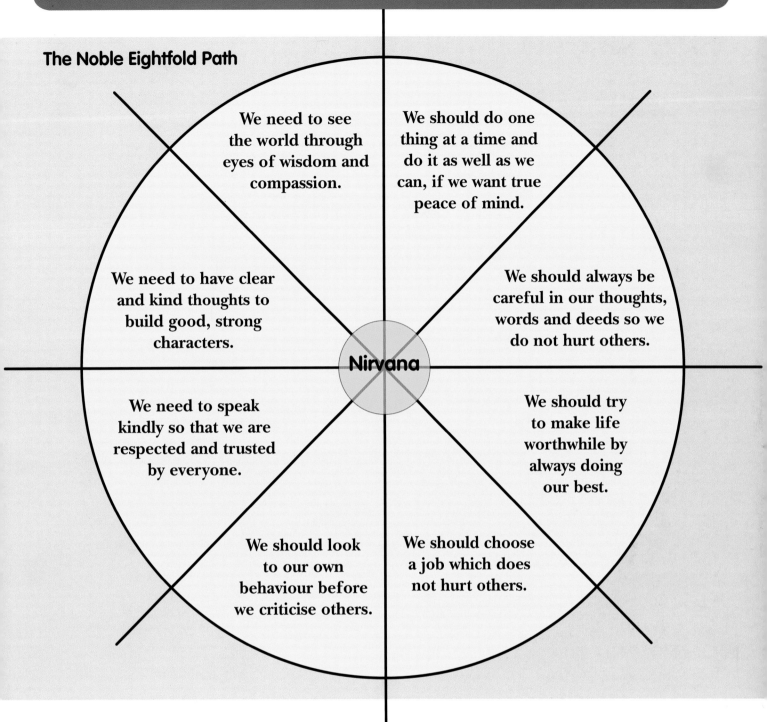

We need to see the world through eyes of wisdom and compassion.

We should do one thing at a time and do it as well as we can, if we want true peace of mind.

We need to have clear and kind thoughts to build good, strong characters.

We should always be careful in our thoughts, words and deeds so we do not hurt others.

Nirvana

We need to speak kindly so that we are respected and trusted by everyone.

We should try to make life worthwhile by always doing our best.

We should look to our own behaviour before we criticise others.

We should choose a job which does not hurt others.

The Triple Jem

When Buddhists have trouble following the Middle Way, they can turn for help to three things, called the **TRIPLE JEM**, or Triple Jewel. The three jems in the Triple Jem are: belief in the Buddha, the **DHAMMA** (the teachings of the Buddha), and the help and wisdom of the worldwide community of Buddhist **MONKS** and **NUNS**, called the **SANGHA**.

Buddhists also follow basic rules of behaviour, which are similar to those found in most other religions. The five most important rules are called the **FIVE PRECEPTS**. They are: do not kill, do not steal, no sexual misconduct, do not lie and do not drink alcohol or take drugs.

Weblink: www.CurriculumVisions.com

The life of Buddha

To understand how Buddhism developed, we have to know about the life of the Buddha, which began some 2,500 years ago.

Siddhartha Gautama, the Buddha, was born around 566 BCE in Kapilavatthu, which is on the present day border of India and Nepal. His father, Suddhodana, was the king and his mother, Maha Maya, was queen.

When Siddhartha was born, a wise man told the king that his son would either be a king or a great HOLY MAN when he grew up.

Because of this, the king was determined to hide anything bad or unpleasant from his son. Siddhartha grew up living in the palace and surrounded by beauty.

▼ This picture is taken from a 17th century Burmese book. It shows the four things the Buddha saw when he left the palace – an old man, a sick man, a corpse and a monk; and the Buddha leaving the palace to search for enlightenment.

He was married when he was 16, and had a child, Rahula, when he was 19. During all of this time he knew only luxury.

The four sights

One day Siddhartha grew bored with the palace and decided to go outside and see a bit of the kingdom. When he left the palace, Siddhartha saw four things that changed his life. He saw an old man, who was bent with age; a sick man; a dead body; and a holy man who had no possessions but was calm.

The first three things convinced Siddhartha that life was actually full of suffering. The fourth thing, the sight of the holy man, showed Siddhartha that the way to find peace and end suffering was to give up his life of luxury.

The search for peace

From that moment on, Siddhartha wanted to give up the comfort of his life in the palace and search for peace. When he was 29, he shaved off his hair, left his loving family and his luxurious possessions behind, and left the palace to become a poor, wandering monk.

Siddhartha travelled for many years, searching for peace. He tried many different ideas, and studied with many different holy men, but nothing he was taught led him to be free from suffering.

Enlightenment

After six years of studying and wandering, the Buddha sat down to think, or **MEDITATE**, under a tree at Bodh Gaya, in north-eastern India. After three days and nights he realised the cause of suffering and how to remove it, and became enlightened. This meant that he was free from the fear of suffering and from the cycle of life, death and rebirth.

From this moment, Siddhartha Gautama was called the Buddha, meaning 'The Awakened One'.

The Buddha teaches

After his enlightenment, the Buddha went to a deer park in Sarnath, near the city of Benares in India, and gave his first sermon, which was about the Four Noble Truths. Many people who heard his sermons decided to become monks and nuns and help spread the Buddha's teachings.

The Buddha taught for the next 45 years. Everywhere he went, people came to listen to him talk about how they could be free from suffering.

The Buddha died in around 486 BCE at the age of 80. Buddhist scriptures tell that he chose the moment of his death and ate some poisoned food. He then lay on his side and meditated until he died.

The Buddhist life

Buddhism is not only practised in a temple, it is part of everyday life.

Buddhists go to **TEMPLES** regularly in order to make **OFFERINGS**, to participate in holiday festivals, and to learn from the monks and nuns, but their faith goes much further than this. It affects their whole lives. When the Buddha taught about the Eightfold Path, he taught that it should influence everything a person does in everyday life. So, Buddhists try to always act in a caring way, to help others and to follow the Buddha's teachings, no matter what they are doing.

Buddhism every day

You can get a clear feeling of how Buddhism affects everyday actions from the following saying of the Buddha: "Life is dear to all living things. They have the right to live the same as we do. We should respect all life and not kill anything."

This tells us that we have a duty to keep the world free from harm for all living things. Most Buddhists are non-violent and many are **VEGETARIAN**, because they feel it is wrong to take a life, any life.

The teachings of Buddha also tell us that we should concentrate and pay attention to each thing we do. This is called **MINDFULNESS**. So, everyday activities like washing clothes, gardening and cooking a meal are as important as 'special' activities like going to a party. Whether you are cleaning your room or getting ready for a party, Buddhism teaches that you should concentrate on what you are doing and make sure that you are following the Eightfold Path as you do it.

▼ Buddhist countries around the world have developed many wonderful and unique vegetarian cuisines.

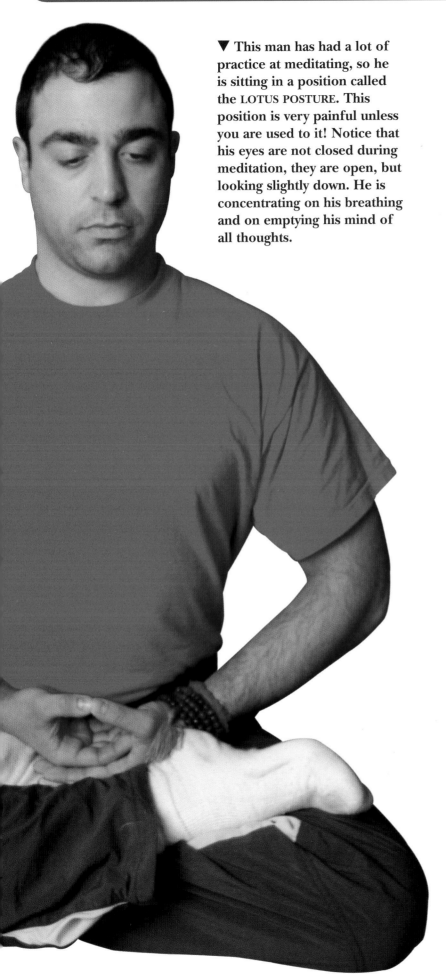

▼ This man has had a lot of practice at meditating, so he is sitting in a position called the LOTUS POSTURE. This position is very painful unless you are used to it! Notice that his eyes are not closed during meditation, they are open, but looking slightly down. He is concentrating on his breathing and on emptying his mind of all thoughts.

Meditation

Meditation is an important part of the Buddhist faith. It is a way of sitting calmly and quietly and concentrating the mind. Meditation clears the mind and helps improve concentration and our ability to think clearly.

Meditation begins by sitting comfortably and focusing on your breathing. You may then concentrate on an object or image in order to clear the mind of everyday thoughts. There are hundreds of different ways to meditate and meditation can last for a few minutes or, with a lot of experience, for many hours.

Many Buddhists meditate every day, often at a quiet time of day. They find that it helps them to stay calm, focused and mindful.

Helping others

The Buddha taught that caring for the world around us is one of the highest goals. Many Buddhists carry out this part of the Buddha's teachings by doing good works. For example, by doing volunteer work, by taking part in peace protests or by building neighbourhood gardens or other peaceful places for everyone to enjoy.

Weblink: www.CurriculumVisions.com

Buddhist devotional worship

Much of Buddhist worship involves learning about the Buddha's teachings and thanking the Buddha in different ways.

Thanking the Buddha

The Buddha is thought of as an enlightened being, not as God, so he is not worshipped. However, Buddhists often perform **RITUALS OF DEVOTION** to confirm their commitment to the **TRIPLE JEM**.

Many Buddhists have a **SHRINE** in their homes with a statue or image of the Buddha in a quiet place. This is where daily rituals of devotion take place. Other people may go to a temple to show devotion.

There are many ways to express devotion. Some Buddhists study Buddhist teachings, make gestures, say prayers, make offerings, meditate, chant or make **PILGRIMAGES** to Buddhist shrines.

▼ Stand facing the Buddha, place the palms together and raise them to the level of the forehead. This shows that your body is dedicated to the Triple Jem (the Buddha, the dhamma and the Sangha).

▼ While standing, lower your hands to just below the mouth to show that everything you say is dedicated to the Triple Jem.

▼ Lower your hands to chest level. This shows that the heart and mind are dedicated to the Triple Jem.

Here are some common ways that people worship through expressing devotion.

Prostration

PROSTRATION is a type of bowing that is usually performed in front of a statue of the Buddha to show respect. There are several different ways to prostrate. The pictures on this page show one way.

Salutation

SALUTATION means greeting, and one of the most common worship practices is to greet monks and nuns, or another Buddhist, with a simple **BOW**.

For this, both hands are placed together in front of the body with the thumbs and fingertips touching and slightly cupped at the palms, and the person bows from the waist. This type of greeting was a way that people showed respect to their parents and other elders when Buddhism began and is still a sign of respect.

▼ Then place your hands together above your head. This shows that your entire being is dedicated to the Triple Jem.

▲ Lower your entire body to the floor, with hands outstretched.

▲ Kneel down and place the palms on the floor.

The entire prostration is repeated three times, once for each part of the Triple Jem.

Weblink: www.CurriculumVisions.com

Making offerings

Buddhists make offerings to the Buddha in order to create good thoughts and feelings (good **KARMA**) and to remind themselves of good qualities, such as giving gifts with a respectful attitude and gratitude.

In Buddhist temples, there is a **SHRINE ROOM** where offerings are made. You can see some of the most common offerings on this spread. Each kind of offering has its own meaning.

Offering of incense

▲ When incense is lit, its fragrance spreads. Buddhists believe that if a person behaves in a good way, then this goodness will also spread. Incense stands for good behaviour and reminds people to behave well towards others.

Offering of fruit

◀ In this picture, incense, fruit and sweets are being offered.

Fruit stands for enlightenment, which is the goal of every Buddhist. Fruit also reminds Buddhists that every action has an effect. Just like every tree has a different type of fruit, and each fruit looks and tastes different, everything we do has a different effect. Sometimes Buddhists also make offerings of sweets or other foods.

Offering of water

▶ Water stands for purity, clarity and calmness. Offerings of water remind people that the Buddha's teachings can help people clean their minds of bad thoughts, such as feelings of anger and hatred. On the shrine, there might be several bowls of water. Sometimes the water is coloured yellow with saffron. The bowls are cleaned every day to make sure they are spotless.

Offering of flowers

▶ The freshness, fragrance and beauty of flowers do not last; fresh and beautiful flowers soon become withered, lose their nice smell and turn black. This reminds people of when the Buddha taught that nothing lasts forever and that we should value what we have now, instead of always wishing for something else.

Offering of light

▶ These people are lighting candles on a shrine in a temple. Light stands for wisdom. Just like a light drives away the dark, the light of wisdom drives away the darkness of ignorance. The light on a Buddhist shrine could be candles, an electric lamp or coloured strings of lights.

▼ These people are chanting in a temple. They are sitting on cushions on the floor in a posture which will help them to concentrate. In front of them are books of mantras (CHANTS) which they will read from. You can see a shrine at the front of the room, with many statues of the Buddha on it. During chanting, it is important to focus your mind on the words and their meaning.

▼ This prayer table is set up for devotional chanting. On the table is a book of prayers, a picture of the Buddha, a string of prayer beads, a bell and a varja.

The picture makes it easier to focus on the Buddha while chanting. The varja, or thunderbolt, is a symbolic weapon. It is a symbol of faith, which is able to cut through anything. When the bell and varja are held together they can mean wisdom.

Taking refuge

Another form of devotion is **TAKING REFUGE** in the Buddha. Taking refuge is purely a mental process of accepting the Triple Jem as one's own supreme guiding principles.

In order to take refuge in the Buddha, a person does a salutation or prostration in front of a shrine, and then repeats the following phrases three times: "I pay homage to the Blessed One, the Worthy One, the Fully Enlightened One. I go to the Buddha for refuge. I go to the dhamma for refuge. I go to the Sangha for refuge."

Another type of purely mental devotional practice is **SHARING MERIT**, where you dedicate the goodness of your life to the benefit of all living beings as well as praying for a particular person.

Chanting

In many Buddhist traditions chanting prayers (sometimes called **MANTRAS**) or the Buddha's teachings is a common way of expressing devotion. The chanting also creates good feelings and attitude (good karma).

While chanting or reciting the Buddha's teaching, worshippers may ring bells and hold devotional objects.

◀ This is a type of prayer wheel. Prayers are written on the outside of the wheel. When the lit candle is placed under the wheel, it spins around, releasing the prayers every time it spins.

Weblink: www.CurriculumVisions.com

Buddhist monks and nuns

Buddhism is guided by its monks and nuns. Their task is to continue the teachings of the Buddha.

Today, Buddha's teachings are taught by **NUNS** and **MONKS**. Monks and nuns may live in a large temple called a **MONASTERY**, and devote their lives to understanding the Buddha's teachings and explaining them to others. But they are also part of the community, teaching and helping with problems.

One way that Buddhists worship is by thanking monks and nuns for their work. Some Buddhists may also worship by becoming a monk or a nun for a short period.

An honour to be a monk or nun

Anyone can become a monk or a nun. In order to do this, Buddhists take part in a ceremony called **ORDINATION**, where they promise to observe a set of rules that affects every part of their lives.

▶ This man is a young novice. Soon he will decide whether or not to become a fully ordained monk.

▲ Monks and nuns do not have possessions and rely on donations. This woman is making a donation of new robes and toiletries at a monastery.

▼ This nun is preparing to perform devotional chanting in a temple. Notice her shaved head. This is a sign that she has given up her former life and is now dedicated to Buddhism.

It is very common in some Buddhist countries for most people to spend some time living at a temple as a **NOVICE** monk or nun. This does not mean the person has decided to dedicate their life to being a monk or nun. Usually, it is an opportunity to learn more about Buddhism.

Living as a novice also allows Buddhists to earn **MERIT**. This is a kind of good karma that will help them to reach Nirvana.

Children may also become novices and live at a temple or monastery for a short period, although some of them may decide later to spend their lives as monks or nuns.

19

Monks and nuns must give up almost all of their possessions, but they still have contact with people outside. In fact, many of them may continue to work outside the temple or monastery, in jobs with non-monks. But they still wear their robes.

Robes and clothing

Monks and nuns give up all of their personal clothing and wear only robes. These robes reflect Buddhist values and traditions. When the ancient Indians looked into the forest they could always tell what leaves were about to fall off the trees because they were yellow, orange or brown. So yellow became the colour of renunciation. Now Buddhist monks wear orange, yellow or brown robes as a constant reminder of the importance of not clinging, and of letting go.

The Buddha and his followers made their robes by sewing together scraps of cloth and dyeing them a common colour.

There are actually three robes – an inner robe, which is a waistcloth for men and a longer skirt for women; an upper robe which covers one arm; and an outer robe, which is used to keep warm in winter. In addition to these, nuns also wear a vest or bodice underneath their robes, and have a thinner robe to wear while bathing (monks wear their waistcloth while bathing).

Rules of living

Monks and nuns are allowed very few possessions. The basics are: robes, belt, shoes, a place to live, an **ALMS BOWL**, medicine and anything needed for personal hygiene. The first monks lived in caves or simple shelters and travelled constantly, but today most live in monasteries or temples.

Buddhist monks and nuns also shave their heads. This is a reminder that they have given up their home life and are a part of the Sangha (worldwide community of monks and nuns). They are no longer concerned with outward beauty, but with developing their spiritual lives.

Monks and nuns must also agree to obey more than 200 **MONASTIC RULES**. These include never having sex, studying each day, and only eating what is given to them or what they have grown themselves. In some places, monks and nuns walk around their neighbourhood every morning and people give them food. In other places, people bring food and other gifts to the monastery or temple.

Monks and nuns do not beg for food, but accept whatever is offered. This practice not only helps the monks and nuns to be humble, but also gives people in the community an opportunity to give to others. Offering food to monks and nuns earns the giver merit, or good karma.

▼▶ These photos show a monastery in Tibet. Tibetan monks are sometimes called lamas. The woman on the right is spinning a prayer wheel in front of a chorten (STUPA), which is a Buddhist symbol and may contain the bones of an important Buddhist lama.

A way of life

Monks and nuns spend much of each day in study and meditation. They may also chant verses from the teachings of the Buddha and recite the monastic rules to remind them of the discipline under which they must live.

They may go out into the community to teach others about Buddhism and do good works.

In some places, monks and nuns may work as school teachers, engineers or in other 'regular' jobs. All of the work of keeping the temple or monastery clean is also done by the monks or nuns.

Everything about this way of life is designed to focus the mind and body on the teachings of the Buddha and on achieving Nirvana.

Weblink: www.CurriculumVisions.com

Written teachings

Buddhist scriptures were written by the disciples of the Buddha.

The Buddha wrote no **SCRIPTURES** himself. He taught by giving talks and by showing people how to meditate. He also taught by example. People could see how the Buddha lived and tried to follow his example.

The Tipitaka scriptures

After the Buddha died, his disciples met to write down his teachings into books. These books contain all of the things the Buddha said and did after he became enlightened and began teaching. These scriptures are called the **TIPITAKA**, or the three baskets, because they contain three main parts, called the Vinaya Pitaka (Discipline Basket), the Sutta Pitaka (Teachings Basket) and the Abhidhamma Pitaka (Higher Teachings Basket). These scriptures are also called the **PALI CANON** because they were written in a language called Pali.

▼ In this picture a monk is holding a modern book which has some of the Buddhist scriptures and prayers translated into English. Some Buddhists use translations of the Buddha's teachings in order to make them easier for people to read. However, many Buddhists also learn Sanskrit or other ancient languages in order to read the scriptures in their original languages.

◀▲ The book this monk is holding is modern, but it has been made the same way as Buddhist books were made in Tibet in ancient times. The words are written in the Tibetan language, and they are handwritten on long, thin sheets of paper. This reminds Buddhists of the first Buddhist books, which were written on long, thin palm leaves. The inset shows a close-up of Tibetan writing. Many Buddhist books are also written in Sanskrit, which is an ancient language spoken in the time of Buddha.

Each of the three parts of the scriptures is, in turn, made up of many individual lessons, or **SUTRAS**. The Vinaya Pitaka includes sutras on the rules by which monks and nuns must live. The Sutta Pitaka contains the Buddha's teachings and other writings about the Buddha, including stories about his life. The Abhidhamma Pitaka is made up of philosophical writings about the Buddhist way of life.

In South East Asia, the scriptures are traditionally written on palm leaves, bound with cords or ribbons and protected with wooden covers. In temples and monasteries, the scriptures are placed on high shelves in a respected part of the building.

Other scriptures

There are many other important books of Buddhist scriptures that record things said by the Buddha or other learned Buddhists. Some of these are the Diamond Sutra, the Heart Sutra, the Lotus Sutra and the Meditation Sutra. These scriptures also teach about Buddhist belief and how to achieve enlightenment.

Weblink: www.CurriculumVisions.com

Learning from symbols

Symbols are used as important teaching tools in Buddhism.

Studying scriptures and listening to talks by monks and nuns are not the only ways that Buddhists learn about Buddhism. They also use symbols, paintings and statues to learn.

In Buddhism you will see many statues and images of the Buddha. These statues are not meant to show exactly what the Buddha looked like in life, instead, they show an idealised version of the Buddha. These images help people to remember important things about the Buddha and his teachings, and events and activities from his life.

Buddha images

Long before the Buddha's time on Earth, Indian wise men said that there were 32 marks, or features, that would be found on a great teacher. The Buddha had all of these, and some of them are usually shown on every image of him.

Some of these are: a wisdom bump on the top of the head, long ear lobes, a spot between the eyes, and 102 symbols on the soles of his feet.

Mudras

Hand gestures, called **MUDRAS**, were also used by wise men in ancient India to convey special meanings. For example, a hand resting gently in the lap was a sign that we must find peace within themselves. Most statues of the Buddha also show him using hand gestures. Buddhists can look at these hand gestures and be reminded of his teachings.

Here are some of the mudras used in Buddhism and their meanings:

Dhammachakra mudra

▼ Dhammachakra in Sanskrit means the 'wheel of dhamma'. The thumb and first fingers of each hand make a circle, which reminds people of the Buddha's first sermon, when he taught about the wheel of dhamma.

The three remaining fingers of each hand are stretched out. The outstretched fingers of the right hand represent the people who listen to the teachings. The extended fingers of the left hand symbolise the Triple Jem. The hands are held in front of the heart, which shows that these teachings come straight from the Buddha's heart.

Dhyana mudra

◀ This stands for meditation. When made with a single hand, the left one is placed in the lap, symbolising wisdom. An alms bowl, symbolising renunciation, may be placed in the open palm. When made with both hands, the right hand is placed above the left, with the palms facing upwards, and the fingers extended.

Vitarka mudra

▼ This mudra symbolises turning the dhamma wheel while meditating. The gesture of the right hand stands for turning the dhamma wheel, while the left hand symbolises meditation.

Bhumisparsa mudra

▲ Bhumisparsa means 'touching the earth'. It is more commonly known as the 'earth-witness' mudra. This mudra reminds people of the time when the Buddha was meditating under the Bodhi tree and he was tempted by evil. He touched the ground and asked the earth to witness that he would not be tempted. The left hand held flat in his lap is a reminder that the Buddha was meditating.

Abhaya mudra

▶ Abhaya in Sanskrit means 'fearlessness'. This mudra symbolises protection, peace and the dispelling of fear. This mudra was probably used from prehistoric times as a sign of good intentions and giving protection. It is also associated with the movement of the walking Buddha and is often used in images showing the Buddha standing.

The Wheel of Life

Buddhists believe that, when a person dies, he or she is reborn into a new body. The endless cycle of rebirth is known as samsara. The only way to escape this cycle is to reach Nirvana. Some Buddhists illustrate the cycle of reincarnation with a painting called the **WHEEL OF LIFE**.

The pictures in the wheel are very scary— they are meant to show people how frightening it can be to have to repeat the cycle forever, and encourage people to escape the cycle by following the Buddha's teachings.

Stupas

After the Buddha died, his body was cremated. His ashes were divided and buried in many traditional burial mounds, called **STUPAS**. Later, many more stupas were built all over the Buddhist world. They did not all contain remains, some contained sacred texts or statues of the Buddha. As Buddhism spread, the shape of the stupa changed from place to place, but every stupa is a reminder of the Buddha and his teachings.

Other symbols

In the early days of Buddhism, symbols were used to teach people the basic ideas of Buddhism.

▲ Stupas are symbols of the Buddha. As Buddhism spread from one country to another, the stupa took on different shapes and names. Some other names for a stupa are: chorten (Tibet and Bhutan), candi (Indonesia), chedi (Thailand), dagoba (Sri Lanka), chedey (Cambodia), tap (Korea), that (Laos), ta (China).

The word pagoda is often used for a stupa that looks like a tower that can be entered and which may be non-religious in purpose.

For example, an image of an elephant might be a reminder of the calm strength of the Buddha.

The umbrella symbolises the protection of the Buddha's teachings.

The conch shell is a symbol of the voice of the Buddha, its low sound is quiet but carries for long distances.

Gardens

Some Buddhist temples and homes have gardens which contain arrangements of stones and sand that has been raked into patterns. These gardens create a feeling of calm and peace. These are common in Japan, where they are called **ZEN** gardens.

The main body of the wheel shows six realms into which one can be reborn: gods, humans, animals, warlike demons, hungry spirits and hell. Each realm is closer to Nirvana than the realm below it. If you do good and follow the Buddha's teachings, you will be reborn into a higher realm each lifetime, eventually reaching Nirvana.

Some believe that these realms are real places. Others believe that they are ways of acting. For example, the realm of warlike demons might mean a lifetime of always being angry and fighting. Or, hell might mean a lifetime which is nothing but suffering.

Buddhist festivals

Festivals are a way for the entire Buddhist community to share and celebrate.

There are many special or holy days held throughout the year by the Buddhist community. Many of these days celebrate the birthdays of enlightened beings, called BODHISATTVAS.

Buddhist festivals are always joyful occasions. On a festival day, people will usually go the local temple or monastery and offer food to the monks and listen to a talk about the dhamma. In the afternoon, they may distribute food to the poor and in the evening they might join in a ceremony of walking around a stupa three times as a sign of respect to the Buddha, dhamma and Sangha. The day may end with chanting of the Buddha's teachings and meditation.

Buddhist New Year

In Thailand, Burma, Sri Lanka, Cambodia and Laos, the New Year is celebrated for three days from the first Full Moon day in April. In other Buddhist countries the New Year starts on the day of the first Full Moon in January.

▼ These worshippers are celebrating Buddhist New Year by placing gold leaf on a statue of the Buddha as a devotional offering. In the background you can see other people leaving offerings of flowers.

▲ Many festival celebrations include traditional music.

The exact day of the Buddhist New Year depends on the country of origin or ethnic background of the people. For example, Chinese, Koreans and Vietnamese celebrate in late January or early February according to their lunar calendar, whilst the Tibetans usually celebrate about one month later.

Vesak or Visakah Puja (Buddha Day)

This festival falls on the Full Moon of the sixth month of the lunar year (around the middle of May on the international calendar). It is one of the most important days for Buddhists because on this day the Buddha was born, became enlightened, and died. All three of these significant events fell on the same day of different years. Visakah Puja is often celebrated with a public talk during the day and a candle lit procession at night to pay respect to the Buddha.

29

Glossary

ALMS Donations of food and other items made to monks and nuns.

ALMS BOWL A bowl that nuns and monks receive offerings in.

BCE This abbreviation stands for 'before common era'. This is another way of writing BC, or 'before Christ', when talking about dates.

BODHISATTVA A being who becomes enlightened but postpones their entrance into Nirvana in order to help others become enlightened.

BOW A way of showing respect by bending at the waist when meeting another person.

BUDDHA The Enlightened or Awakened One. The founder of Buddhism. The word comes from the Sanskrit *budh*, which means 'to awaken'.

BUDDHISM The name of the religion of people who follow the teachings of the Buddha.

CHANT A way of worshipping which involves saying certain phrases aloud in a set rhythm.

DHAMMA The teachings of the Buddha. It is sometimes written as dharma.

DHAMMA WHEEL An illustration of the way to follow the Buddha's teachings.

ENLIGHTENMENT Understanding the truth of life, becoming free from ignorance. Complete elimination of all negative aspects of the mind and perfection of all positive qualities.

FIVE PRECEPTS The five rules of conduct given by the Buddha to his disciples: no killing, no stealing, no sexual misconduct, no false speech, no intoxicants.

FOUR NOBLE TRUTHS The first teachings spoken by the Buddha, they are the truth of suffering, the cause of suffering, the end of suffering, and the path leading to the end of suffering.

HOLY MAN In ancient India there were many people who travelled around, living simply and without possessions, and preaching.

KARMA A Sanskrit word for the cosmic law of cause and effect: every physical or spiritual deed has its long-range consequences. So, if you do good in this life, you will build up good karma for the next life and your next life will be better.

LOTUS POSTURE A cross-legged sitting posture used in advanced meditation. The position is supposed to resemble a lotus flower and encourages proper breathing, concentration and physical stability.

MANTRAS A sacred word or phrase which is repeated over and over in certain Buddhist rituals.

MEDITATE/MEDITATION A method of calming and training the mind.

MERIT A person can gain insight, power or energy (merit) by performing a good action. Buddhists can also gain merit through chanting, giving alms and other good deeds.

MIDDLE WAY The path in life prescribed by the Buddha, the path between extremes.

MINDFULNESS The state of being aware of every action you are doing, no matter how small or unimportant.

MONASTERY A large temple, usually with many monks or nuns in residence. Monasteries may have many buildings, including temples and stupas.

MONASTIC RULES The rules by which monks and nuns must live.

MONK A man who has given up everything and decided to devote his life to Buddhism.

MUDRA A hand gesture with a special meaning.

NIRVANA An everlasting state of great joy and peace. Literally, the 'unbinding' of the mind from passion, aversion' and delusion, and from the entire cycle of death and rebirth.

NOBLE EIGHTFOLD PATH The Buddha's prescription for ending suffering. It is made up of eight parts: right views, right thought, right speech, right action, right livelihood, right effort, right mindfulness and right concentration.

NOVICE A monk or nun in training, or a person who is living as a monk or nun only temporarily.

NUN A woman who has given up everything and decided to devote her life to Buddhism.

OFFERING A way of showing respect and devotion to the Buddha by giving gifts with special meanings.

ORDINATION A ceremony after which a person is a full monk or nun.

PALI CANON Buddhist scriptures written in an ancient language of India, called Pali.

PILGRIMAGE A trip to a place of special importance.

PROSTRATION A way of bowing where you lower your entire body to the ground in order to show respect.

REINCARNATION The idea that each person is born into the world over and over again.

RITUALS OF DEVOTION Ways that Buddhists show their respect to the Buddha and his teachings.

SALUTATION A word which means 'greeting'. This is a way of greeting someone who you respect.

SANGHA The community of Buddhist nuns and monks.

SANSKRIT An ancient language of India that the Buddhist sutras were written in.

SCRIPTURES Holy books of the Buddha's teachings.

SERMON A talk or teaching given by a learned or holy person.

SHARING MERIT A way of sharing good thoughts and good karma with others. One way is to meditate and think good things about the person or people you want to share merit with.

SHRINE A type of altar which holds images or statues of the Buddha. This is used as a focus for Buddhist devotional practices.

SHRINE ROOM A room in a temple or a monastery which contains a shrine.

SIDDHARTHA GAUTAMA The name that the Buddha was born with. The Buddha is not a god, but an ordinary person who became enlightened.

STUPA A shrine which reminds Buddhists of the burial mounds that the Buddha's ashes were placed in. A stupa often has a dome shape.

SUTRAS A sacred text, such as the Buddha's teachings.

TAKING REFUGE Accepting, in your mind, that the dhamma, the Buddha and the Sangha are very important to you. This may involve a ceremony where certain phrases are spoken, or it may only take place in your mind.

TEMPLE A place where Buddhists go to learn about Buddhism, to talk with monks or nuns and to practice rituals of devotion.

TIPITAKA The 'three baskets', a collection of the Buddha's written teachings.

TRIPLE JEM (TRIPLE JEWEL) The Buddha, the dhamma and the Sangha.

VEGETARIAN A person who does not eat any meat. Some vegetarians do not eat any animal products, such as eggs and milk, at all.

WHEEL OF LIFE A way of illustrating the six worldly states of rebirth: gods, warlike demons (asuras), humans, animals, hungry spirits and hell-beings.

ZEN A type of Buddhism which is common in Japan and China. It involves spending long periods of time in meditation. A Zen garden often contains plants, sand and stones which are arranged in certain ways and are used in meditation.

Index

Curriculum Visions

Curriculum Visions is a registered trademark of Atlantic Europe Publishing Company Ltd.

◆ **Atlantic Europe Publishing**

Dedicated Web Site
There's more about other great Curriculum Visions packs and a wealth of supporting information available at our dedicated web site:

www.CurriculumVisions.com

First published in 2005 by
Atlantic Europe Publishing Company Ltd
Copyright © 2005
Atlantic Europe Publishing Company Ltd

Authors
Brian Knapp, BSc, PhD, and Lisa Magloff, MA

Religious Adviser
Lama Zangmo, Kagyu Samye Dzong, London

Art Director
Duncan McCrae, BSc

Senior Designer
Adele Humphries, BA, PGCE

Acknowledgements
The publishers would like to thank Kagyu Samye Dzong for their kind help and advice, without which this book would not have been possible. For more information, please contact them at: Kagyu Samye Dzong Tibetan Buddhist Centre, Carlisle Lane, Lambeth, London SE1 7LG.
Tel: 020 7928 5447. Fax: 020 7633 9339.
Web site: www.samye.org/london

Photographs
The Earthscape Editions photolibrary, except page 8 *British Library* and page 21 *ShutterStock*.

Illustrations
David Woodroffe

Designed and produced by
Earthscape Editions

Printed in China by
WKT Company Ltd

Buddhist faith and practice
– Curriculum Visions
A CIP record for this book is available from the British Library

Paperback ISBN 1 86214 460 5
Hardback ISBN 1 86214 461 3

This product is manufactured from sustainable managed forests. For every tree cut down at least one more is planted.

All rights reserved. No part of this publication may be reproduced, stored in a retrieval system, or transmitted in any form or by any means, electronic, mechanical, photocopying, recording or otherwise, without prior permission of the Publisher.